My Bible Book

Alan and Linda Parry

Contents

The Beginning

Noah and the Ark

Joseph and His Coat

Baby Moses

Baby Jesus

The Farmer and the Seed

Jesus Is Alive!

Paul Meets Jesus

The Beginning

In the beginning there was nothing

except God.

One day God made light.

That gave us day and night.

The next day God made the sky

with its white clouds.

On the third day God made the land

with its flowers and trees.

On the fourth day God made the sun,

the moon and the stars.

On the fifth day the sea was
filled with fishes,

and the birds crowded the sky.

God made the animals on the sixth day,

every different kind.

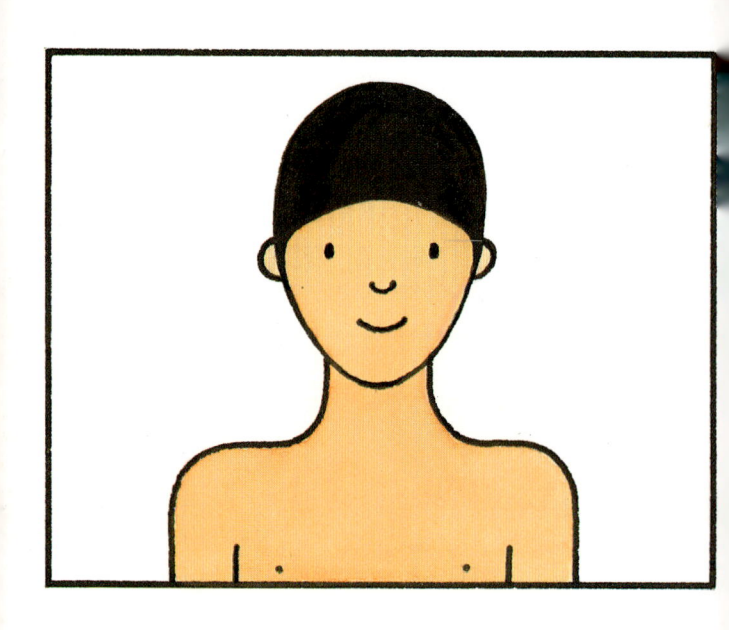

Then God made a man and woman.

They were like God.

The man and woman lived together in a beautiful garden

where they were very happy.

Then God looked at what was made

and was pleased.

God rested on the seventh day

and made it special.

You can read about how the world was made in Genesis 1:1-2:4.

Noah and the Ark

Noah loved God.

He was the only man who did.

All the other people were bad,

and God decided to start the world again.

He told Noah to build a huge boat

that would be called an ark.

Noah took his family into the ark

and two of every animal
and bird.

Then it started to rain.

And it rained

and rained.

It rained for forty days and nights

till the water was everywhere.

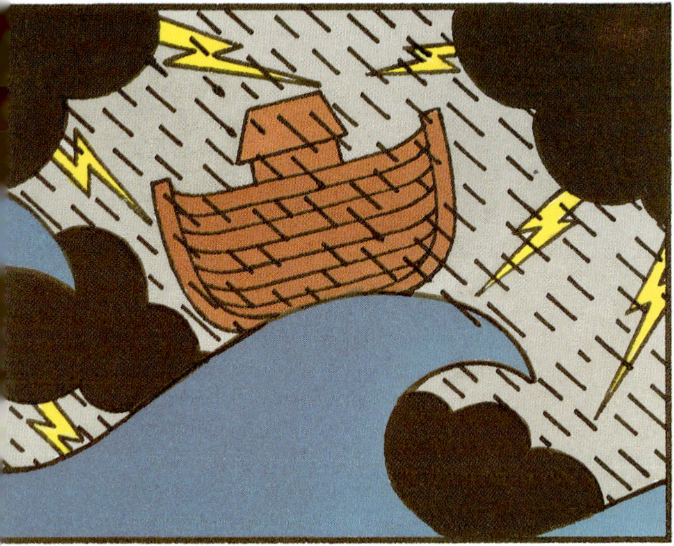

Finally it stopped.

The ark landed on a mountaintop.

Noah sent out a dove, and it came back with a leafy branch.

So the earth was getting dry.

Finally, all the animals and Noah left the ark.

And Noah thanked God for saving them.

God put a rainbow in the sky

And said there would never be another flood like this one.

You can read about Noah and the ark in Genesis 6:5-9:17.

Joseph and His Coat

This is Joseph with his new coat.

It's a beautiful coat.

Joseph's brothers were jealous.

They wanted to get rid of him.

So they threw him into a pit.

Then they sold him as a slave to some traders.

They took him to a faraway country called Egypt.

A man called Potiphar bought Joseph.

But Potiphar's wife told lies about him,

and he was thrown into prison.

Pharoah, the king of Egypt,
dreamed two strange dreams.

Nobody could tell him what they meant.

But God showed Joseph the meaning of dreams,

so Pharoah called Joseph out of prison.

"The dreams," Joseph said, "mean you will have seven years with plenty to eat and seven years with nothing."

Pharoah put Joseph in charge of the food supplies.

Joseph's brothers came to
Egypt to buy food.

At first he pretended he was angry with them.

They didn't know he was their brother!

Then he told them who he was.

They were so happy to see him again, they all came to live with him.

You can read about Joseph
in Genesis 37 and 39-45.

Baby Moses

Pharoah was the king of Egypt.

He was very angry.

He gave orders to his soldiers

to throw all baby Hebrew boys
into the river.

When Moses was born,

his mother didn't want him to
be hurt.

She made him a little basket

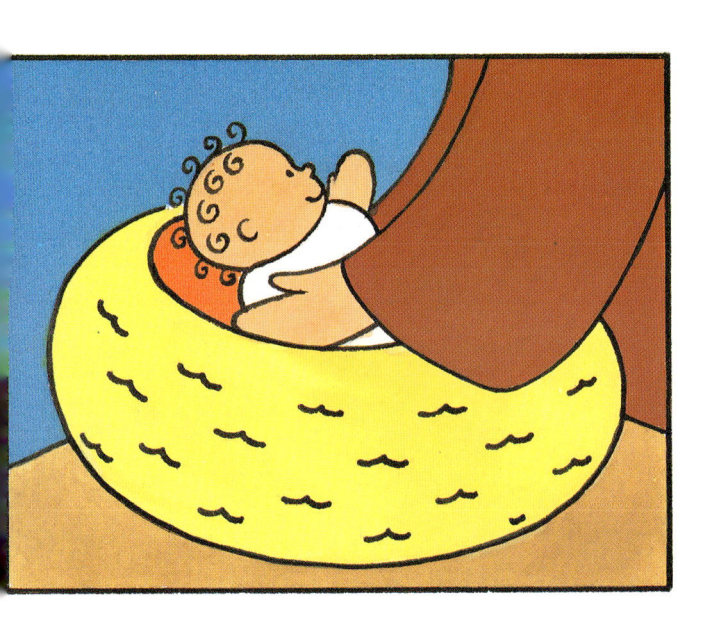

that wouldn't let the water in.

She hid the basket on the river

and Moses' older sister watched it.

Then a princess came to swim in the river.

She was the Pharoah's daughter!

She saw the little basket in the reeds

and asked her maid to fetch it.

Moses was crying,

and Pharoah's daughter felt sorry for him.

She decided to look after
Moses herself,

but she needed a nurse to help her.

Moses' sister ran to get their mother,

and she became his nurse.

So Moses grew up in the
Pharoah's palace

and often saw his own family too.

You can read about Baby Moses
in Exodus 1:7-2:10.

Baby Jesus

This is Mary.

This is Joseph.

This is the angel Gabriel.

God sent him to Mary.

Gabriel said Mary would soon have a baby, God's Son.

Then Gabriel went to Joseph.

He told Joseph to name the baby, Jesus.

They went on a long journey
to Bethlehem.

There was no room for them in the inn.

Jesus was born that night in a stable.

Mary wrapped him up and laid him in a manger.

In the hills there were
shepherds with their sheep.

Suddenly angels appeared.
The shepherds were frightened.

One angel said, "Don't be afraid.

We have good news. The Lord Jesus has been born."

The shepherds went to look for Jesus.

They found him in the stable with the animals.

They praised God for the wonderful things they had seen.

Far away in the East, a star appeared.

Some wise men saw it and followed it to Bethlehem.

They brought precious gifts and gave them to Jesus.

They were very happy to have found him.

You can read about the birth of Jesus in
Matthew 1:18-2:23,
and Luke 1:5-2:20.

The Farmer and the Seed

This is the farmer.

He is planting the seed.

Some seed falls on the path.

The birds soon eat it up.

Some seed falls among the rocks.

The plants grow quickly in the shallow soil.

But when the hot sun shines

they die, because they have no roots.

Some seed falls into thorns

that choke the little plants.

But some seed falls into
good soil,

and grows up big and strong.

Jesus told this story.

He said that the seed was the Word of God.

Some people don't accept
God's Word;

Then the Word is snatched away, like seed on the path.

Some people don't trust Jesus enough;

Then the Word shrivels up, like seed on the rock.

Some people put other things before God,

choking the Word, like the seed in the thistles.

Some people truly follow Jesus;

They are the good soil, and grow up as God's people.

You can read about the farmer and the seed in Matthew 13:4-8, 18-23;
Mark 4:3-8, 14-20;
and Luke 8:5-8, 11-15.

Jesus Is Alive!

Terrible news in Jerusalem –

the Lord Jesus had died on the cross.

Jesus' disciples were sad.

What would they do without him?

His friends, Joseph and
Nicodemus,

took the body down from the cross.

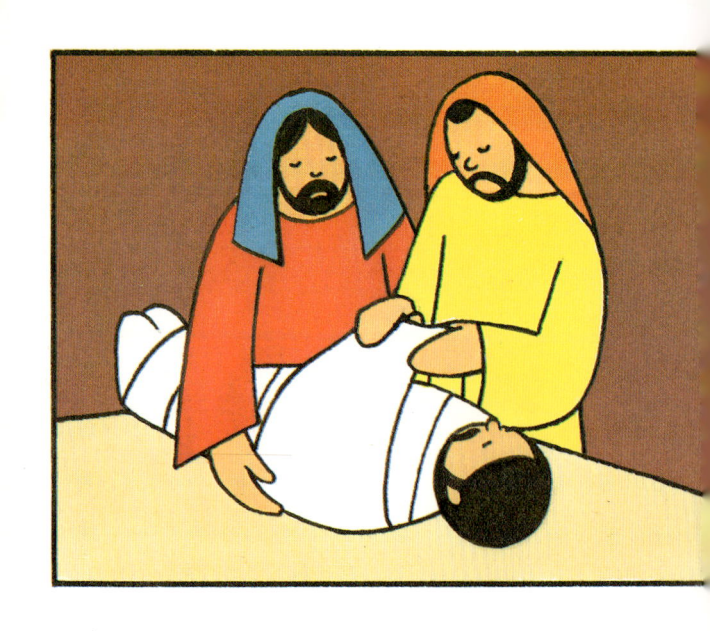

They wrapped it in a linen cloth

and laid it in a nearby tomb.

A heavy stone was rolled across the entrance.

Early in the morning a woman called Mary came to the tomb.

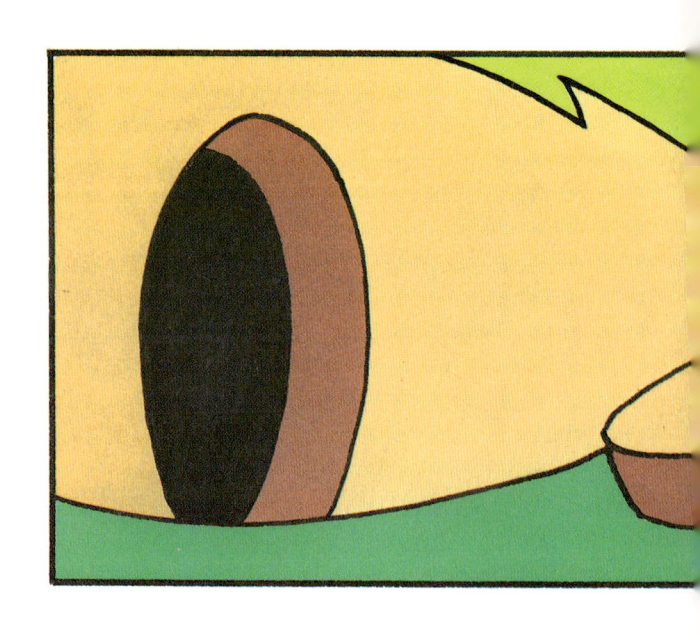

The stone had been rolled away!

She ran to tell the disciples.

Two of them ran to the tomb.

They looked inside – it was empty!

They went home, wondering what had happened.

But Mary stood outside, crying.

Then, when she looked up,

she saw Jesus standing there!

Jesus went to see the disciples.

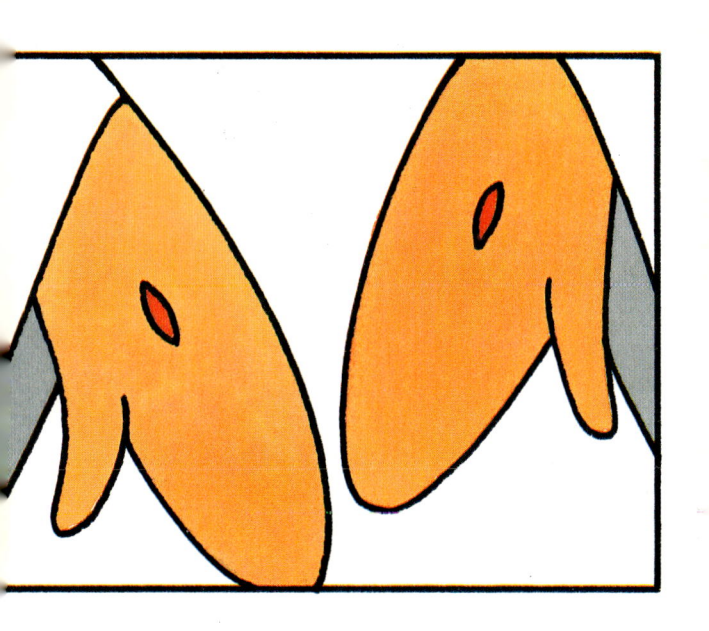

He showed them the marks in his hands.

The disciples weren't sad anymore.

"Jesus is alive!" they shouted.

You can read about Jesus coming back to life in John 19:38-20:20.

Paul Meets Jesus

Paul hated Christians.

They believed Jesus was the Son of God.

He thought they were wrong!

He put lots of them into prison.

When he had put into prison all he could find,

Paul set out for a town called Damascus, to find some more.

On the way,

a brilliant light suddenly shone down on him.

He fell to the ground, and Jesus spoke to him.

"Why do you hate those who believe in me?" Jesus asked.

Then Paul knew that the Christians were right!

Jesus was the Son of God.

When Paul stood up, he was blind!

His friends led him on to Damascus.

He was blind for three days.

He didn't eat or drink, but prayed to God.

In a dream, Jesus spoke to a man called Ananias.

He told Ananias to go and help Paul.

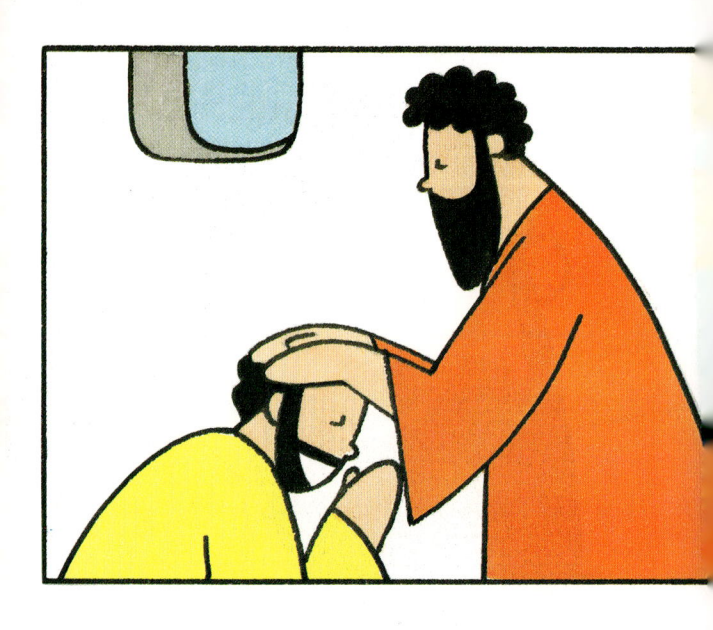

So Ananias went to Paul and prayed with him.

Then Paul could see again!

Paul was baptized and became a Christian.

He set off at once to teach others about Jesus.

You can read about Paul in Acts 8:3; 9:1-22;22:4-16; and 26:9-18.